MATCH!

JOKE
BOOK!

Another MATCH! title from Macmillan Children's Books

MATCH! Incredible Stats & Facts!

MATCH!

JOKE BOOK!

ILLUSTRATED BY RUSS CARVELL

MACMILLAN CHILDREN'S BOOKS

First published 2016 by Macmillan Children's Books
an imprint of Pan Macmillan
20 New Wharf Road, London N1 9RR
Associated companies throughout the world
www.panmacmillan.com

ISBN 978-1-5098-2499-1

Text copyright © Macmillan Children's Books 2016
Branding copyright © Bauer Consumer Media Limited 2016
Compiled by Dan Newman

13

A CIP catalogue record for this book is available from
the British Library.

Designed by Tony Fleetwood
Printed and bound by CPI Group (UK) Ltd, Croydon CR0 4YY

Contents

What goes stomp, stomp, stomp, squelch?

An elephant with wet football boots.

How can you stop moles digging up the football pitch?

Hide their spades.

What's large, grey and carries a trunk and two pairs of football boots?

An elephant that's just joined the team.

Why did Rovers win 12–0?

They had an elephant in goal.

Why can't horses play football?

Because they've got two left feet.

Why was the centipede no use to the football team?

He never got on the pitch until half-time – it took him so long to lace up his boots.

Why are there fouls in football?

The same reason there are ducks in cricket.

Two flies were playing football in a saucer. One said to the other, 'We'll have to do better than this; we're playing in the cup next week!'

What happened when a herd of cows had a football match?

There was udder chaos.

What's the difference between a flea-ridden dog and a bored football spectator?

One's going to itch; the other's itching to go.

A man was walking his dog past Villa Park when the final score was announced over the speakers – Aston Villa had lost 1–0. Immediately the dog rolled on to its back and stuck all four legs in the air. 'That's impressive,' said a fan. 'What does she do when we win?' The man thought for a moment. 'I'm not sure,' he said. 'I've only had her six months.'

Why did the chicken run on to the pitch?

Because the referee blew for a fowl.

MY DOG DOESN'T LIKE FOOTBALL.

She's a boxer.

WHY DID THE CHICKEN GET A RED CARD?

For persistent fowl play.

What did the
bumblebee
striker say?

'Hive scored!'

'Coach, why is there an onion
tied to the crossbar?'
'To keep the training ground
free of elephants, lad.'
'Elephants? There aren't any
elephants round here!'
'That's because it works.'

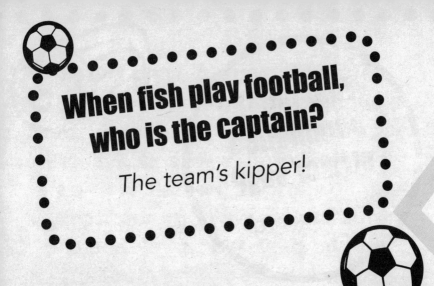

When fish play football, who is the captain?

The team's kipper!

THAT CHICKEN PLAYS BEAUTIFUL FOOTBALL.

He's poultry in motion.

What position did the ducks play in the football team?

Right and left quack.

The ants were playing the elephants at football. The game was going well, and the elephants were leading 4–0 when the ants' star striker got the ball. He was dribbling his way up the pitch, until he only had the elephant left back to beat. The elephant lumbered up and trod on the ant, squashing him flat. The referee stopped the game. 'What do you think you're doing?

Do you call that sporting, hurting another player?'

'Sorry,' the elephant replied. 'I didn't mean to hurt him. I was just trying to trip him up.'

What was the monkey in the team especially good at?

Banana shots.

WHY DID THE FOOTBALLER'S DOG RUN AWAY FROM HOME?

Doggone if I know!

Two fleas were leaving a football match when it started to rain. 'Shall we walk?' asked the first flea. 'No,' said the second, 'let's take a dog.'

WHAT DO YOU GET IF YOU CROSS A GORILLA WITH A FOOTBALLER?

I don't know, but when it tries to score a goal no one tries to stop it!

Which fox is brilliant at football?

Brazil Brush.

Who ran out on the pitch when a player was injured and said, 'Miaow'?

The first-aid kit.

What should you get a spider for Christmas?

Four pairs of football boots.

Why don't elephants play football?

Because they can't get shorts that fit.

QUICK PASSES

What can light up a dull evening?

A football match.

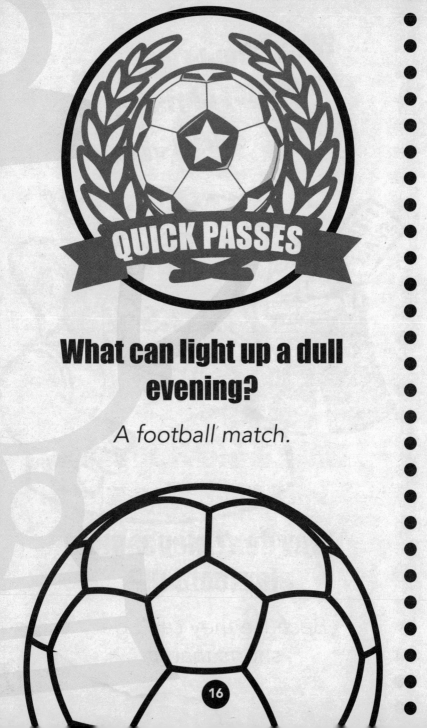

16

When is a football coach not a football coach?

When it turns into the ground.

Why are mummies no good at football?

They're too wrapped up in themselves.

What's the best thing to do when a football is in the air?

Use your head.

What did the left football boot say to the right football boot?

'Between us we should have a ball.'

19

Which part of the team bus is the laziest?

The wheels – they're always tyred.

What's the difference between the Prince of Wales and a throw-in?

One's heir to the throne; the other's thrown in the air.

Why was the pitch in such a bad mood?

It was fed up of being treated like dirt.

Who wears the biggest boots in the England team?

The player with the biggest feet.

When is a footballer like a grandfather clock?

When he's a striker.

When is a footballer like a baby?

When he dribbles.

How do you stop a hot and sweaty footballer from smelling?

Put a peg on his nose!

What did the ball say to the footballer?

'I get a kick out of you.'

How can a footballer stop his nose running?

Put out a foot and trip it up.

WHAT TWO THINGS SHOULD A FOOTBALLER NEVER EAT BEFORE BREAKFAST?

Lunch and dinner.

What does a football do when it rolls to a halt?

Looks round.

What's black and white and wears dark glasses?

A football in disguise.

What can a footballer never make right?

His left foot.

How do ghost footballers keep fit?

With regular exorcise.

WHY DID THE MANAGER FLOOD THE PITCH?

He wanted to bring on a sub.

What's yellow, has 22 legs and peels off at half-time?
Banana United.

Why did the potato go to the match?
So it could root for the home team.

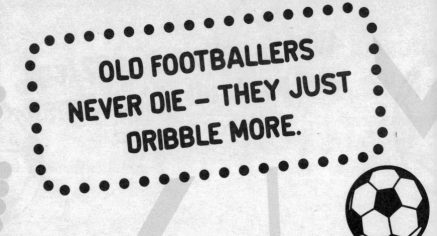

OLD FOOTBALLERS
NEVER DIE – THEY JUST
DRIBBLE MORE.

A man went to meet the members of a vegetable football team. 'This stick of celery is our goalkeeper, the carrots are our centre forwards and the onions are our defenders,' explained his host. 'And what's that one over there, telling everyone else what to do?' he asked, pointing to a mud-covered vegetable that was lounging around. 'Oh, him?' replied the host. 'He's our coach potato.'

How many people can you fit into the Nou Camp when it's empty?

Only one.
After that it isn't empty any more.

What position did Cinderella play in the football team?

Sweeper.

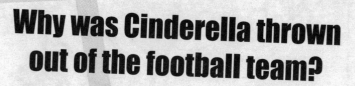

Why was Cinderella thrown out of the football team?

Because she kept running away from the ball.

Which goalkeeper can jump higher than the crossbar?

All of them – crossbars can't jump.

Why do ghosts play football?
For the ghouls, of course.

Who delivers mail to footballers?
The goal-post man.

What do you call a press photographer taking pictures of the match?

A flash guy.

Did you hear the story of the peacock that played football?

It's a beautiful tail.

What was wrong with the footballer whose nose ran and feet smelt?

He was built upside down.

What gloves can a keeper see and smell but not wear?

Foxgloves.

What's the difference between a gutter and a poor keeper?

One catches drops; the other drops catches.

What's the difference between a goalkeeper who's asleep and one who's awake?

With some keepers it's difficult to tell!

The inventor of the red card died at the weekend, and the funeral's next week.

He'll get a good send-off.

Don't ever play football against a university Chemistry department. It always ends up in a massive argument about the oxide rule.

Why did the footballer hold his boot to his ear?

Because he liked sole music.

What do you call an Englishman in the semi-final of the World Cup?

The referee.

Which part of a football pitch smells the nicest?

The scent-er spot.

What's a keeper's favourite snack?

Beans on post.

What's black and white, and black and white, and black and white?

A Newcastle fan rolling down a hill.

What's the difference between a footballer and an overweight jogger?

One runs in short bursts, the other runs in burst shorts.

Which part of a football stadium is never the same?

The changing rooms.

There are three types of footballer: those who can count, and those who can't.

Why did the footballer bring a ball of string on to the pitch?

He was hoping to tie the game.

FOOTBALLERS ARE THE ONLY PEOPLE WHO CAN LOOK STYLISH WHILE DRIBBLING.

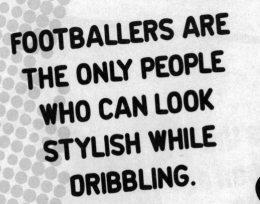

What do footballers like to drink?

Penal-tea.

What's the difference between the England team and a teabag?

The teabag stays in the cup longer.

Why was the ruler no good at football?

He just couldn't measure up.

What belongs to a footballer but is used more by other people?

His name.

How can a footballer make more of his money?

If he folds up a note he'll find it in creases.

43

Why did the millionaire footballer have no bathroom in his house?

He was filthy rich.

Why did the footballer eat little bits of metal every day?

It was his staple diet.

Why can't a car play football?

Because it's only got one boot.

What do jelly babies wear when they play football?

Gumboots.

What kind of leather makes the best football boots?

No one knows, but banana peel makes the best slippers.

What's the difference between an oak tree and a tight football boot?

One makes acorns, the other makes corns ache.

Why did the football decide to stop playing the game?

It was tired of being kicked around.

What runs all the way round a football pitch but never moves?

A fence.

TICKET

Where's the best place to buy a football shirt when you're in America?

New Jersey.

Which coconut-flavoured biscuit plays for Man. United?

Wayne Macarooney.

Have you heard about the footballer with three legs?

He's always one step ahead.

Did you know boots that close with Velcro cost more than ones with laces?

What a rip-off.

THE TOILET
FACILITIES AT MOST
STADIUMS ARE VERY
ORDINARY.
THEY'RE BOG
STANDARD.

YOU NEVER KNOW HOW
LONG A PROFESSIONAL
CAREER WILL LAST, SO IT'S
IMPORTANT FOR FOOTBALLERS
TO PUT SOMETHING AWAY FOR
A RAINY DAY.
AN UMBRELLA, MAYBE.

The England team got into trouble on the flight out to the World Cup.

They kept running up the wing.

Why wasn't the goalkeeper feeling well?

Because he'd forgotten to take his gloves off.

Who's in goal when the ghost team plays football?

The ghoulie, of course!

What wears out football boots but has no feet?

The ground.

Why did the footballer put seed in his boots?

He had pigeon toes.

How short can a footballer's shorts get?

They'll always be above two feet.

SIGN ON A NEW SPORTS-KIT SHOP: DON'T GO ELSEWHERE TO BE ROBBED – TRY US FIRST!

Why does a professional footballer always put his right boot on first?

It would be silly to put the wrong boot on, wouldn't it?

What runs around all day and lies still at night with its tongue hanging out?

A football boot.

What does a footballer part with but never give away?

His comb.

What can a footballer keep even if he does give it to others?

A cold!

Why did the footballer stand on his head?

He was turning things over in his mind.

Why was the snowman no good playing in the big match?

He got cold feet.

Why did the big-headed player throw a bucket of water on the pitch when he made his debut?

He wanted to make a big splash.

What does a footballer do if he splits his sides laughing?

He runs until he gets a stitch.

IF IT TAKES 20 PLAYERS HALF AN HOUR TO EAT A HAM, HOW LONG WILL IT TAKE 40 PLAYERS TO EAT HALF A HAM?

That depends on whether they are professionals or 'am-a-chewers'.

KNOCK ON THE DRESSING-ROOM DOOR

Knock, knock.
Who's there?
Waiter.
Waiter who?
Waiter minute while I tie my bootlaces.

Knock, knock.
Who's there?
Saul.
Saul who?
Saul over when the final whistle blows.

Knock, knock.
Who's there?
Wooden.
Wooden who?
Wooden it be great if we won the Cup?

Knock, knock.
Who's there?
Farmer.
Farmer who?
Farmer birthday I got a new pair of football boots.

Knock, knock.
Who's there?
Nana.
Nana who?
**Nana your business
who we put in goal.**

Knock, knock.
Who's there?
Deceit.
Deceit who?
Deceit of your shorts is all muddy.

Knock, knock.
Who's there?
Omar.
Omar who?
**Omar goodness,
what a shot!**

Knock, knock.
Who's there?
Police.
Police who?
Police let me play with your new football.

SCHOOL FOOTBALL

'I CAN'T RUN, CAN'T SHOOT, CAN'T ORIBBLE AND I'M NO GOOD IN GOAL.'

'Why don't you give up football?'

'I CAN'T – IT'S MY BALL.'

'Are there any holes in your football shorts?'

'No, of course not.'

'Then how do you get them on?'

ANDY CAME OFF THE PITCH LOOKING MISERABLE, AND SLUNK INTO THE DRESSING ROOM. 'I'VE NEVER PLAYED SO BADLY BEFORE,' HE SIGHED.
'OH,' ANSWERED HIS CLASSMATE. 'YOU'VE PLAYED BEFORE, HAVE YOU?'

TEACHER: *What form are you in, lad?*

JAKE: *Well, I scored two goals last Saturday.*

TEACHER: *And why were you late for school today, Tom?*

TOM: *I was dreaming about a football match and they went into extra time.*

DAD:
How did this window get broken?

HARRY:
Er, my football took a shot at goal while I was cleaning it.

MUM: Ethan! It's time to get up! It's 8.15!

ETHAN: Who's winning?

MATHS TEACHER: Who can explain to me what net profit is?

ALEX: When your team wins 6–0.

'WERE YOU ANY GOOD AT FOOTBALL, DAD?'
'WELL, I ONCE RAN DOWN THE PITCH FASTER THAN ANY OTHER PLAYER. AND IF I EVER FIND OUT WHO PUT THAT WASP IN MY SHORTS I'LL MURDER THEM!'

67

Darren and Sharon were playing football one evening, trying to kick the ball into a goal marked out on a wall.

'We'd better go – it's getting dark,' said Darren. 'And we haven't scored a single goal yet.'

'Let's miss a few more before we go,' said Sharon.

A woman was frying some eggs for breakfast. Suddenly her son burst into the kitchen.

'Careful! Careful!' he yelled. 'Put in some more butter! Oh nuts! You're cooking too many at once. TOO MANY! Turn them! TURN THEM NOW! We need more butter. Oh no! Where are we going to get more BUTTER? They're going to STICK! Careful! CAREFUL! I said CAREFUL! You NEVER listen to me when you're cooking! Never! Turn them! Hurry up! Are you crazy? Have you lost your mind? Don't forget to salt them. You know you always forget to salt them. Use the salt! USE THE SALT! THE SALT!'

His mother stared at him. 'What's wrong with you? You think I don't know how to fry a couple of eggs?'

The son calmly replied, 'I just wanted to show you what it feels like when I'm trying to play football.'

A scout was talking to a young player who had applied for a tryout with the club. 'Can you kick with both feet?' asked the scout. 'Don't be silly!' said the player. 'If I did that, I'd fall flat on my bum!'

Two kids were kicking a brand-new ball around when their mum came home.
'Where did you get that from?' she asked.
'We found it,' replied her youngest child.
'Are you sure it was lost?' asked their mother.
'Oh yes,' said her other child. 'They're still looking for it.'

'So what do you want for Christmas, Ashley?'

'I really want those new boots I showed you at the weekend. I've had my eye on them for ages.'

'Remind me – how much are they?'

'Eighty quid, Dad.'

'Keep your eye on them, then. Because you're never going to get your feet in them.'

'Dad, I think I might have been picked for a position in the school team!'

'Really? That's great, son. But why do you only think you've been picked? And what position?'

'Well, the team hasn't been announced yet. But I overheard the coach talking to my teacher, and he said that if I was in the team I'd be a great drawback.'

'STOP THE BALL! STOP THE BALL!' YELLED THE PE TEACHER TO THE YOUNG KEEPER. 'OH NO! WHY DIDN'T YOU STOP IT?' 'I THOUGHT THAT WAS WHAT THE NET WAS FOR,' SNIFFED THE POOR BOY.

A kind lady found a little boy sitting crying on the pavement. 'What's the matter, young man?' she asked. 'It's my birthday,' sobbed the lad. 'And I got a new football, and some boots, and a Man. United shirt, and a video, and . . .'
'If you got all those lovely things, why are you crying?' asked the lady. 'I'm lost,' sobbed the boy.

Two boys were walking past a house surrounded by a high wall when the owner came out holding a football. 'Is this your ball?' he demanded.

'Er, has it done any damage?' asked the first boy.

'No,' said the owner.

'Then it's ours,' said the second boy.

It was Christmas time, and a little boy was being asked by his teacher about the Three Wise Men. 'Who were they?' asked the teacher.

'They were footballers,' replied the little boy.

'Whatever do you mean?' asked the teacher.

'Well, the carol says, "We three kings of Orient are . . ."'

PARK-KEEPER: Why are you boys playing football in the trees?

TOM: Because the sign says no ball games on the grass.

'Why don't you like your new football coach?'

'Because he told me to play in goal for the present, and he didn't give me a present!'

At one point during a football match,
the coach called one of his
twelve-year-old players aside and asked,
'Do you understand what cooperation is?
What a team is?'
The boy nodded.
'Do you understand that what matters
is whether we win or lose together
as a team?'
The boy nodded again.
'So,' the coach continued, 'I'm sure you
know that when a corner is given, you
shouldn't argue, swear or call the ref rude
names. Do you understand all that?'
Again the boy nodded.
He continued, 'And when I take you off so
another boy gets a chance to play, it's not
good sportsmanship to call your coach a
"useless pudding", is it?'
Looking slightly ashamed by now,
the boy agreed.
'Good,' said the coach. 'Now go over
there and explain all that to your mum.'

Two young footballers were talking about the illnesses and accidents they'd had.
'Once I couldn't walk for a year,' said the first.
'When was that?' asked the other.
'When I was a baby,' replied the first.

'Mum, can I go out and play?'

'What, with those holes in your socks'?

'No, with Billy next door – he's got a new football.'

'You've got your boots on the wrong feet.'

'I can't have – these are the only feet I've got.'

MUM: Why are you crying?

JACOB: Kyle's lost his football boots.

MUM: But if he's lost his boots, why are you crying?

JACOB: Because I was wearing them when he lost them.

'Robert! Scrape that mud off your football boots before you come in the house.'

'But I haven't got my boots on, Mum. I went out in my socks.'

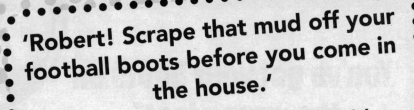

'I can't find my football boots, Mr Williams. I've looked everywhere for them.'

'Are you sure these aren't yours? They're the only pair left.'

'Quite sure. Mine had snow on them.'

Chris was sent home from school at lunch for not bringing his football kit. When he returned in the afternoon he was soaked through. 'Why are you all wet?' asked the PE teacher.

'Sir, you said I must play football in my kit, so I went home to fetch it but it was all in the wash.'

'Pull up your socks – they're all wrinkled.'

'But I'm not wearing any socks.'

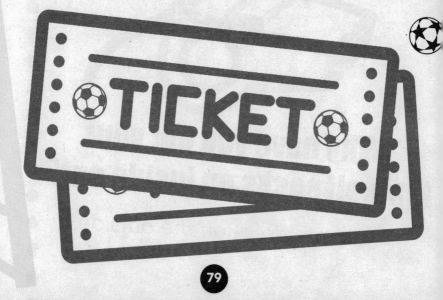

'I wish I were in your boots.'

'Why?'

'Mine have holes in them.'

OLDER BROTHER:
Have you got your football boots on yet?

YOUNG BROTHER:
Yes . . . all except one.

'Why have you got your football socks on inside out?'

'There are holes on the outside.'

MOTHER: Why are you taking the baby's bib out with you, Sean? I thought you were going to football practice?

SEAN: Yes, but the coach said we'd be dribbling this week.

PE TEACHER: Now, Lucas, I'm trying to show you how to make a tackle. I wish you'd pay a little attention.

LUCAS: I'm paying as little as I can.

'I had an argument with my sister. I wanted to watch football on TV and she wanted to watch a film.'

'What film did you see?'

NEIGHBOUR: I'll teach you to kick footballs at my greenhouse!

KEIRAN: I wish you would – I keep missing!

Two boys were trespassing on the local football pitch and the groundsman came out and shouted at them. 'Didn't you see that sign?' he yelled. 'Yes, but it said "Private" at the top so we didn't think we should read any further,' replied the boys.

PE TEACHER: Now, Blake, you promised to practise hard at your football, didn't you?

BLAKE: Yes.

PE TEACHER: And I promised to punish you if you didn't practise?

BLAKE: Yes. But I don't mind if you break your promise.

KNOCK ON THE DRESSING-ROOM DOOR

Knock, knock.
Who's there?
Thermos.
Thermos who?
Thermos be a better team than this!

Knock, knock.
Who's there?
Wanda.
Wanda who?
Wanda buy a new football?

Knock, knock.
Who's there?
Gladys.
Gladys who?
Gladys Saturday – we can go to the match.

Knock, knock.
Who's there?
Justin.
Justin who?
Justin time to see us lose!

Knock, knock.
Who's there?
Tyrone.
Tyrone who?
Tyrone bootlaces.

Knock, knock.
Who's there?
Norma Lee.
Norma Lee who?
Norma Lee I play in goal but today I'm at left back.

Knock, knock.
Who's there?
Althea.
Althea who?
Althea later, after the game.

FOOTBALLER: *I've had an idea that might help us win a few matches.*

CAPTAIN: *Good. When are you leaving?*

MR GREEN:

I've been invited to join my firm's football team. They want me to play for them very badly.

MR BROWN:

In that case, you're ideal for it.

CAPTAIN: You should have been at training at 8.30!

PLAYER: Why, what happened?

After the match the team was in the dressing room when the trainer came in and asked if anyone had seen his glasses. 'Yes,' replied one of the players. 'They were out on the pitch.'
'Then why didn't you bring them in?' asked the trainer.
'I didn't think you'd want them after everyone had trodden on them,' replied the player.

DEFENDER:

When is it your birthday?

KEEPER:

2nd June.

DEFENDER:

Which year?

KEEPER:

Every year.

'DID YOU HEAR OUR TEAM NOW PLAYS THE NATIONAL ANTHEM BEFORE EACH MATCH?'
'ARE THEY REALLY THAT PATRIOTIC?'
'NO. THEY PLAY IT TO MAKE SURE EVERYONE IN THE TEAM CAN STAND UP.'

Why did the joker in the team climb on to the cafe roof at the celebration dinner?

He'd heard the meal was on the house.

The team's coach-driver went to a garage. 'Can you have a look at my bus? I think the engine's flooded,' he told the mechanic.
'Is it on the road outside?' asked the mechanic.
'No, it's at the bottom of the canal,' replied the driver.

'Wasn't the captain angry when you said you were leaving the team next month?'
'Yes. He thought it was this month.'

The manager gathered the team after a dismal start to the season. 'Right, lads, we need to get back to basics. What I'm holding in my hands is a football, and the object of the game—'
'Whoa, slow down, boss,' called one player. 'You're going too fast.'

Did you hear the club was burgled last night? Though all they took were the soap and towels from the players' dressing room.
The dirty crooks.

'Coach, have you got any ideas how I can improve my penalties?'

'Yes, I've been watching and you're standing too close to the ball . . . after you've kicked it.'

'So, boss, have you noticed any improvement in me this week?'

'Yeah . . . you've had a haircut, haven't you?'

Our team manager won't stand for any nonsense. Last game he caught a couple of fans climbing over the stadium wall. He was furious. He grabbed them and yelled, 'Now you get back in there and watch the rest of the game.'

Our keeper's rubbish.

The only thing he's caught so far this season is a cold.

'WHY DO YOU CALL OUR CAPTAIN "CAMERA"?'

'Because he's always snapping at me.'

If it takes twenty men six months to build a grandstand at our ground, how long would it take forty men to build it?

No time at all, because the twenty men have already completed it!

The club advertised for a handyman, and Mr Perkins came for an interview. 'Well, Mr Perkins,' asked the manager, 'what qualifications do you have for this job? Are you handy?'
'I reckon so,' replied Mr Perkins.
'I only live next door.'

'THAT NEW PLAYER IS AN ABSOLUTE WONDER.'

'Why do you say that?'

'BECAUSE I LOOK AT HIM AND WONDER IF HE'S EVER PLAYED BEFORE!'

MANAGER: This dressing room is disgusting! It looks like it hasn't been cleaned for a month!

CLEANER: Don't blame me. I've only been here for a fortnight.

'What's your team like?'

'Well, there's always a long queue at the ground – trying to get out!'

The leading striker kept looking at the grandstand.
'Are you thinking of kicking the ball up there? asked his teammate.
'My mother-in-law's sitting there,' explained the striker.
'But even you won't hit her from here,' replied his teammate.

'While Darren was taking a shower after the match someone stole all his clothes.'
'Oh dear! What did he come home in?'
'The dark!'

SCOUT: *Your number six looks as if he could be a good footballer if his legs weren't so short.*

MANAGER: *They're not that short! They both reach the floor.*

YOU KNOW, FOR A MOMENT THERE I REALLY THOUGHT WE WERE IN WITH A CHANCE OF WINNING.

THEN THE GAME STARTED.

A thief broke into the football club and stole all the entrance money – but why did he take a shower before he left?

So he could make a clean getaway.

STRIKER: I had an open goal but still I didn't score! I could kick myself.
MANAGER: I wouldn't bother. You'd probably miss.

Liam was nervous the first time he played for the team, and when they stopped for half-time he asked the captain, 'I suppose you've seen worse players.'
The captain scratched his head.
'I said, I suppose you've seen worse players,' persisted Liam.
'I heard you the first time,' replied the captain. 'I was just trying to remember.'

'Boss, I don't like these boots. Can I change them?'
'What's wrong with them?'
'They're sticking their tongues out at me.'

'Hey, boss! You know that jigsaw puzzle I was doing? You'll never guess – I've finished it, and it only took me six months!'
'What's so great about taking six months to do a jigsaw?'
'Because on the box it said "Three to six years".'

TWO TRAINEES RAN ON TO THE TRAINING GROUND ONE MORNING. 'OH NO, LOOK,' SAID ONE. 'A DEAD BIRD.' THE OTHER ONE LOOKED UP AT THE SKY AND SAID, 'WHERE?'

Our striker was coming out of the stadium after a typical match.
'Can I have your autograph?' asked a small boy.
Trying to get away from him, the footballer replied, 'I really don't play football.'
'I know,' said the boy. 'But I'd like your autograph anyway.'

FOOTBALLER: You should be ashamed, giving me such a poultry salary.
MANAGER: You mean 'paltry'.
FOOTBALLER: No, I mean 'poultry' – it's chicken feed.

Why did the player come to the ground dressed in diving gear? He'd been told he might be needed as a sub.

'How old is your keeper?'
'Approaching thirty.'
'From which direction?'

NOBODY EVER PASSED THE BALL TO CARL, AND HE WAS MOANING IN THE DRESSING ROOM THAT HE MIGHT AS WELL BE INVISIBLE. 'WHO SAID THAT?' ASKED THE CAPTAIN.

It was a warm day for football and the striker kept missing his shots. At half-time he said, 'Phew! What couldn't I do with a long, cold drink!' His captain looked at him thoughtfully. 'Kick it?' he asked.

YOUNGER PLAYER:
How old are you?

OLDER PLAYER:
Thirty-two. But I don't look it, do I?

YOUNGER PLAYER:
No, but you used to.

'Watch out when tackling him. He's got a bum like concrete. If you aim too high, you could hit rock bottom.'

It's really upsetting – someone cleaned our boots with bleach. It's eaten away all the bottoms. In fact it's sole-destroying.

CAPTAIN:
Why are you late for training?

PLAYER:
I sprained my ankle.

CAPTAIN:
That's a lame excuse.

A weedy little man wanted to get fit enough to play football, so he bought a big book on body building and worked hard on the exercises for three months. A friend asked him if it had had any effect. 'Oh yes,' he replied. 'I can now lift up the book.'

'That new striker is a man who's going places!'
'Yeah, and the sooner the better!'

Do you like our new captain?'
'I can't complain. Let's face it, I daren't!'

'Our coach always thinks twice before speaking.'
'Yes, so he can think up something really nasty to say!'

'We tried playing in those new paper shirts last week.'
'What are they like?'
'Tear-able.'

INSURANCE AGENT: This is a very good policy, sir. We pay up to £1,000 for broken arms and legs.

FOOTBALLER: But what do you do with them all?

KNOCK ON THE DRESSING-ROOM DOOR

Knock, knock.
Who's there?
Aladdin.
Aladdin who?
Aladdin the street's waiting for you to come out and play football.

Knock, knock.
Who's there?
Kerry.
Kerry who?
**Kerry me off the pitch – I
think my leg's broken.**

Knock, knock.
Who's there?
Albie.
Albie who?
**Albie home
straight after
the match.**

Knock, knock.
Who's there?
Felix.
Felix who?
Felix-cited about going to the Cup tie.

Knock, knock.
Who's there?
Ammonia.
Ammonia who?
Ammonia little boy and I can't run as fast as you.

Knock, knock.
Who's there?
Money.
Money who?
Money hurts since I twisted it on the pitch.

Knock, knock.
Who's there?
Venice.
Venice who?
Venice the next away match?

Knock, knock.
Who's there?
Harvey.
Harvey who?
**Harvey going to have another game
before lunch?**

FANATICAL FOLLOWERS

What do you do if you're too hot at a football match?

Sit next to a fan.

A football fan was driving the wrong way down a one-way street when he was stopped by a policeman who asked where he was going.
'To the match,' he answered.
'But I must be too late – everyone else is coming back.'

OLD FAN: *At last I've finally got my new hearing-aid.*

FRIEND: *Does it work well?*

OLD FAN: *Half-past three.*

A TOURIST VISITING LONDON STOPPED A MAN CARRYING A FOOTBALL AND ASKED, 'HOW DO I GET TO WEMBLEY?' 'PRACTISE,' WAS THE REPLY.

FIRST FAN: Are you superstitious?

SECOND FAN: No.

FIRST FAN: Good. Then lend me £13 to get into the match.

'Every night I dream about football – of running down the pitch, passing the ball, avoiding tackles . . .'

'Don't you ever dream about girls?'

'What? And miss a chance at goal?'

Newcastle has some unusual fans – for instance, there are fifteen sumo wrestlers who come to every home game. Yeah, they've got a big following.

It was a boring and disappointing match, with very little action.
'I'm surprised the spectators don't yell at them,' said a man in the stand.
'Difficult to shout while you're asleep,' replied his friend.

Manchester United was playing Chelsea at Stamford Bridge. A man wearing a red-and-white rosette walked up to the ticket office and asked the price of admission.
'Twenty pounds, sir,' said the attendant.
'Here's ten pounds,' replied the man. 'There's only one team worth watching.'

'I had a try-out once. The coach said I'd make a great footballer if it weren't for two things.' 'What were they?' 'My left foot, and my right foot.'

'Our team's doing so badly that if they win a corner they do a lap of honour.'

'I've worked it out, and we've still got a slim chance of avoiding relegation if we can just win nine out of our last three games.'

The FA has set up a support line for fans that are distressed by the recent performance of their team. The number is **0800 10 10 10**. All calls are charged at your local rate. That number again: **0800**, won nothing, won nothing, won nothing.

'Football, football,' sighed Mrs Roberts. 'That's all you think of. I bet you don't even remember when we got married.'
'I certainly do,' said Mr Roberts. 'It was the day Arsenal beat West Ham 6–1.'

A KEEN FAN WAS ABOUT TO BECOME A FATHER FOR THE FIRST TIME, BUT ON THE DUE DATE HIS TEAM WAS PLAYING AWAY. 'IT'S NOT A PROBLEM, DARLING,' HE TOLD HIS WIFE. 'I'M GOING TO RECORD IT. THEN I CAN WATCH THE BIRTH WHEN I GET BACK FROM THE GAME.'

A Sheffield man was asked why his car was painted red on one side and blue on the other. 'Because I can't decide whether to support United or Wednesday,' he explained.

What are the noisiest fans called?

Foot-bawlers.

BOSS: I thought you wanted the afternoon off to see your dentist.

MR BROWN: That's right.

BOSS: Then how come I saw you leaving the football ground with some bloke?

MR BROWN: That was my dentist.

MRS GREEN: My husband's found a hobby he can stick to at last.
MRS WHITE: What's that?
MRS GREEN: He spends all evening glued to the football on TV.

Three Newcastle fans were talking about the sad state of their club.

The first fan said, 'I blame the manager: if we could sign better players, we'd be a great club.'

The second fan said, 'I blame the players: if they made more effort, I'm sure we would score more goals.'

The third fan said, 'I blame my parents: if I had been born in Manchester, I'd be supporting a decent team.'

Two fans were queuing to get in to Goodison Park.

'I wish I'd brought my piano with me,' said one.

'Your piano? Why on earth would you want to bring a piano here?'

'Because I left the tickets on it.'

Simon took his seat in the third row of Old Trafford for the big football match.

Upon looking around, he was surprised to see his young neighbour, Dave, in the front row.

'Hi, Dave!' he called out.

Dave turned round. 'Hi, Simon!' he called back.

'How did you get a front-row ticket?' Simon asked.

Dave answered, 'From my older brother.'

Simon asked, 'Where is he?'

Dave answered, 'At home looking for his ticket!'

How many Liverpool fans does it take to change a light bulb?

None – they just like to talk about how good the old light bulb was.

How many Man. United fans does it take to change a light bulb?

Three – the first to change the light bulb, the second to buy the commemorative Manchester United Light Bulb Change DVD and the third to drive the other two back to London.

How many Wigan fans does it take to change a light bulb?

Both of them.

MAN. UNITED FANS WATCH MAN. UNITED TV . . . CHELSEA FANS WATCH CHELSEA TV . . . ARSENAL FANS WATCH ARSENAL TV . . . LIVERPOOL FANS WATCH THE HISTORY CHANNEL!

'Do you think it will rain for the match this afternoon?'
'That depends on the weather, doesn't it?'

'Did you hear that the police are searching the football crowd for a man with one eye called McTavish?'
'What's his other eye called?'

Two fans were discussing their packed lunches.
'What have you got?' asked Jake.
'Tongue sandwiches,' Sam replied.
'Ugh, I couldn't eat something that had come out of an animal's mouth.'
'What have you got, then?' asked Sam.
'Egg sandwiches.'

'Can you telephone from a football match?'

'Of course I can tell a phone from a football match – there are lots of people at a football match.'

YOUNG FAN: *Did you say you learned to play football in six easy lessons?*

STAR PLAYER: *Yes. It was the 600 which came afterwards that were difficult!*

Wayne Rooney:
Where were you born?
Matteo Darmian: *In Italy.*
Wayne: *Which part?*
Matteo: *All of me, of course!*

What's Wayne Rooney's favourite supper?

Fish and chipping.

How do you hire a Premier League footballer?

Stand him on a chair.

What has legs like John Terry, a face like John Terry and arms like John Terry, yet isn't John Terry?

A photograph of John Terry.

A MAN REALIZED THAT HIS NEW NEIGHBOUR WAS A FAMOUS FOOTBALLER.
'I'VE SEEN YOU ON THE TV, ON AND OFF,' HE SAID.
'AND HOW DO YOU LIKE ME?' ASKED THE PLAYER.
'OFF,' REPLIED HIS NEIGHBOUR.

How can you make Peter Crouch short?

Get him to lend you all his money.

What do Lionel Messi and a magician have in common?

Both do hat-tricks.

How does Ronaldo change a light bulb?

He holds it in the air, and the world revolves around him.

MICHAEL OWEN IS GOING TO RELEASE A PERFUME NEXT YEAR. HE'S CALLING IT 'MY COLOGNE'.

John Terry was walking through the park with a pig on a lead. 'That's unusual, where did you get him?' asked a passer-by. 'I won him in a raffle,' said the pig.

After moving to Man. City, Raheem Sterling celebrated by buying some really fast chocolates.

Ferrari Rocher.

Then he bought loads of lamb chops.

Just because he's minted.

TO CELEBRATE A GOAL, ROMELU LUKAKU LIKES TO LIE DOWN ON THE GRASS AND ROTATE HIS BODY TO PROPEL HIMSELF SIDEWAYS.. BUT THAT'S JUST THE WAY HE ROLLS.

At the end of last season Kasper Schmeichel spent two weeks sitting on a large hardback book.

It was his annual holiday.

What's as tall as Peter Crouch but weighs nothing?
His shadow.

SCOTT SINCLAIR SPENT AGES LOOKING FOR A HOUSE AFTER MOVING TO ASTON VILLA. IT *WAS* HIS HOUSE; HE JUST COULDN'T REMEMBER WHERE HE LIVED.

Harry Kane was dreaming about training when the coach said, 'On your marks, get set, go!' He woke up with a start.

Old Tony had been retired from the game for many years, but he still liked to tell people how good he'd once been.

'They still remember me, you know,' he said. 'Only yesterday, when I was at Old Trafford, there were lots of press photographers queuing to take my picture.'

'Really?' said a disbelieving listener.

'Yes. And if you don't believe me, ask Wayne Rooney – he was standing next to me.'

Two footballers were about to retire.

'Apparently there's only one way of making money honestly,' said the first.

'What's that?' asked the second.

'I knew you wouldn't know,' retorted the first.

HALLOWEEN HEROES

Pablo ZOMBIE-leta
(Manchester City)

BAT Ritchie *(Bournemouth)*

Virgil FANG Dyke *(Southampton)*

Wilfried BONY
(Manchester City)

SATAN Baines *(Everton)*

Luka Mod-WITCH
(Real Madrid)

Yannick BOO-lasie
(Crystal Palace)

FRANKENSTEIN Ribery
(Bayern Munich)

TEAM SPIRIT

Which football team never meets before a match?

Queen's Park Strangers.

Which football team should you not eat in a sandwich?

Oldham.

In a theatre a magician was introducing his act. 'I will show you the mysteries of the Orient,' he said.

A voice from the audience called out, 'But what about Reading? They could do with a bit of magic as well!'

Someone has broken into Newcastle United's trophy room and stripped it clean. Police have asked people to look out for anyone trying to sell six dusty shelves and a black-and-white carpet.

What's the difference between Aston Villa and a vase of flowers?

You can imagine a vase of flowers on top of a table.

CLUBS RELEASE ALL SORTS OF BRANDED PRODUCTS FOR FANS. NEWCASTLE EVEN SELLS A BLACK-AND-WHITE-STRIPED OXO CUBE TO CELEBRATE THEIR CURRENT FORM. IT'S CALLED THE LAUGHING STOCK.

Health and Safety regulations mean the chefs at Anfield must always cook Chinese food in pairs – they must never cook on their own. There's a sign up to remind them: 'You'll Never Wok Alone.'

Bolton have got a tough game this weekend. They've got to play football.

In 2006 the architect was showing the Arsenal team around the new Emirates stadium. 'I think you'll find it's completely flawless,' he said proudly. 'What do we walk on, then?' asked Theo Walcott.

Which football team comes out of an ice-cream van?
Aston Vanilla.

Which London team keeps its boots in the fridge?
Tottenham Coldspur.

WHICH FOOTBALL TEAM SPENDS ALL ITS SPARE TIME IN NIGHTCLUBS?
Blackburn Ravers.

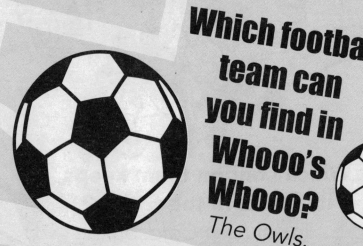

Which football team can you find in Whooo's Whooo?
The Owls.

Why is a scrambled egg like Villa in the 2015 FA Cup Final?

They're both beaten.

WHAT TEAM IS GOOD IN AN OMELETTE?

Best Ham.

A delivery truck lost control and spilled Italian sauce all over the pitch at Selhurst Park.

They've called Pesto Control.

Jurgen Klopp only accepted the Liverpool manager's role if they could also give the job as mascot to his brother, Klippity.

ARSENAL BOUGHT ARSENE A HUGE HELIUM BALLOON TO CELEBRATE HIS BIRTHDAY, BUT HE WASN'T HAPPY.

It didn't go down very well.

The main gates at Anfield are made of sponge.
You can't knock that.

The Everton team found someone had left lumps of clay all over their dressing room.
They didn't know what to make of it.

154

WHEN MANAGER GARY BOWYER LEFT BLACKBURN, AS A PARTING GIFT THEY GAVE HIM . . . A COMB.

Kilmarnock are interested in Belgian defender Mark de Man. Apparently, they are also interested in his compatriots, striker Skor de Gaulle and keeper Bloek de Schott.

To save time, Leeds United has already sacked their next three managers.

The chairman of the FA was wheeling his shopping trolley across the supermarket car park when he noticed an old lady struggling with her shopping. He stopped and asked, 'Can you manage, dear?' The old lady replied, 'No way. You got yourself into this mess, I'm not taking on the England job!'

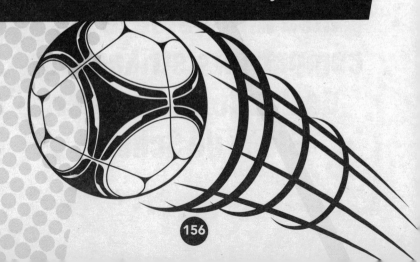

As I was walking home from school last week I noticed a West Brom season ticket nailed to a tree. I thought to myself, I'm having that! Because you can never have enough nails, can you?

What's the difference between West Ham and an albatross?
An albatross has got two decent wings.

What is the difference between Aston Villa and the Bermuda Triangle?
The Bermuda Triangle has three points.

What's the difference between Arsenal and a mosquito?
A mosquito stops sucking.

How many Sunderland managers does it take to change a light bulb? No one knows – none has been there long enough for a bulb to burn out.

WHY ARE ARSENAL STRIKERS LIKE GRIZZLY BEARS?

Every autumn they go into hibernation.

I'm not saying they're lazy at Yeovil Town, but the fire alarm has a snooze button.

WHO LET THE DOGS OUT!

Emile HUSKY *(Bolton)*

John TERRIER *(Chelsea)*

SPANIEL Sturridge *(Liverpool)*

Ross BARK-ley *(Everton)*

Harry CANINE *(Tottenham)*

PUP Guardiola *(Manchester City)*

Wilfried BONE-y *(Manchester City)*

FRUITY FAVOURITES

Fer-MANGO *(Manchester City)*

PEAR Mertesacker *(Arsenal)*

Aaron LEMON *(Everton)*

KIWI Sung-Yeung *(Swansea)*

Ibrahim APPLE-ay *(Stoke City)*

HALF-TIME

A young football fan of Southend
Wrote in rhyme; several verses
he penned,
Of their triumphs and glory,
Their total history –
It drove all his friends round the bend.

A YOUNG FOOTBALL FAN
FROM QUEBEC
ONCE WRAPPED BOTH HIS
FEET ROUND HIS NECK.
THOUGH HE TRIED HARD,
HE GOT
TIED UP IN A KNOT,
AND NOW HE'S AN
ABSOLUTE WRECK.

A striker who came from Devizes
Did little to help win the prizes.
When asked for a reason,
He said, 'Well, this season
My boots were of two different sizes.'

A football pitch groundsman
from Leeds
Went and swallowed a packet
of seeds.
In less than an hour
His head was a flower
And his feet were all covered
in weeds.

A precious young striker from Spain
Said he hated to play in the rain.
One day in a muddle
He tripped in a puddle
And ended up washed down
the drain.

THERE WAS A
YOUNG PLAYER FROM CREWE
WHO NEVER FOUND THAT MUCH TO DO.
FOR AN HOUR OR SO
HE RAN TO AND FRO
AND AFTER HE RAN FRO AND TO.

A young man who once played
for Dover
Had no shirt, so he wore a
pullover.
But the thing was too long
And he put it on wrong
So all he could do was fall over.

KNOCK ON THE DRESSING-ROOM DOOR

Knock, knock.
Who's there?
Buster.
Buster who?
Buster Old Trafford, please.

Knock, knock.
Who's there?
Colin.
Colin who?
Colin and see me after the match.

Knock, knock.
Who's there?
Yolande.
Yolande who?
Yolande me some money to get into the match and I'll pay you back next week.

Knock, knock.
Who's there?
Mister.
Mister who?
Mister bus, that's why I'm late for the match.

Knock, knock.
Who's there?
Harriet.
Harriet who?
Harriet all my sandwiches, now I'm too weak to play!

MEDICAL MISHAPS

Someone threw a pillow on to the pitch and hit Mikel Arteta. Doctors say he's suffering from mild concushion.

Jordan Henderson tripped over a bottle of Omega-3 capsules during training. Luckily his injuries are only super-fish-oil.

'I've just been to the doctor and he said
I can't play football.'
'Oh? When did he see you play?'

The doctor
was giving the team a
medical. 'Breathe in and
out three times,' he said to
one of the players.
'Are you checking my lungs?'
asked the player.
'No, I'm cleaning my glasses,'
replied the doctor.

A footballer had been hit very hard on his knee, which had swollen up enormously. 'If it gets bigger, I shan't be able to get my shorts on,' he told the doctor.

'Don't worry – I'll write you a prescription,' said the doctor.

'What for?'

'A skirt.'

The winger got stretchered off, saying his leg was agony. The doctor heard a tiny voice coming from the man's knee, and when he put his stethoscope on it, he heard, 'Lend us a tenner, lend us a tenner.'

'My ankle hurts too,' said the winger, so the doctor listened there as well. Again there was a little voice, saying, 'Lend us a tenner, lend us a tenner.'

'I know what's wrong,' said the doctor. 'Your leg's broke in two places.'

Sergio Aguero went to see the team doctor. 'I don't know what's wrong with my eyes, Doc. Wherever I look I keep seeing a ladybird spinning in circles.' 'Yeah, don't worry about it. There's a bug going round.'

Olivier Giroud was stretchered off in a lot of pain and taken straight to the doctor. 'It's bad, Doc,' he said through gritted teeth. 'When I touch my knee, it hurts. When I touch my stomach, it hurts. When I touch my elbow, it hurts. Everywhere I touch, it hurts!' 'I've worked out the problem,' said the doctor. 'You've broken your finger.'

Why did the man become
a marathon runner instead
of a footballer?
The doctor told him he had
athlete's foot.

Did you hear about the footballer who had to lose weight? He went on a coconut and banana diet. He didn't lose any weight, but he couldn't half climb trees!

Why did the doctor write on the footballer's toes?

To add a footnote.

DOCTOR: How's your broken rib?
FOOTBALLER: I keep getting a stitch in my side.
DOCTOR: That's good; it shows the bones are knitting.

FOOTBALLER: I've a terrible pain in my right foot. What should I do?
PHYSIOTHERAPIST: Kick the ball with your left.

GOALKEEPER:
Doctor, I can't sleep at night.
DOCTOR:
How long has this been going on?
GOALKEEPER:
About a year.
DOCTOR:
You haven't slept for a year?
GOALKEEPER:
Oh, I can sleep during matches, just not at night.

FIRST FOOTBALLER:
How did you manage to break your leg?

SECOND FOOTBALLER:
See those steps down to the car park?

FIRST FOOTBALLER:
Yes?

SECOND FOOTBALLER:
I didn't.

**Frank Lampard went
for a medical check-up.**
'I'm a bit worried my
eyesight's not what it
was, Doc.'
'You might be right,
love. This is the
canteen.'

The goalkeeper was so short-sighted he couldn't see the ball until it was too late. A doctor friend prescribed carrots to help his eyesight. The keeper ate lots of carrots, but went back to the doctor a month later, saying he still couldn't catch the ball because every time he ran he now tripped over his ears.

ALEXIS SANCHEZ WAS HIT ON THE HEAD BY A SET OF TINY BONGOS.

He's got mild percussion.

'That ointment the doctor gave me to rub on my knee makes my hands smart.' 'Then why don't you rub some into your head?'

THAT'S NOT CRICKET?

UMPIRE Mertesacker *(Arsenal)*

Thibaut CAUGHT-ois *(Chelsea)*

Leroy FOUR *(Queens Park Rangers)*

Jeffrey SLIP *(Leicester City)*

Gareth BAILS *(Real Madrid)*

SEASIDE SKILLS

Aaron Ram-SEA *(Arsenal)*

SANDY Carroll *(West Ham)*

Jason PUNCH & JUDY
(Crystal Palace)

Toni CRUISE *(Real Madrid)*

Theo Walc-HOT *(Arsenal)*

Arouna ICE-CREAM CONE
(Everton)

SURF-io Aguero *(Man. City)*

Jonjo SHELL-vey *(Newcastle Utd)*

MEET THE WAGS

'That footballer annoys me.'
'But he's not even looking at you.'
'That's what's annoying me!'

What happened when the boy footballer married a girl footballer?

People said it was a perfect match.

'Are you still engaged to that footballer?'

'No, my feelings changed towards him, so I broke off the engagement.'

'I see you're still wearing the engagement ring, though.'

'Well, my feelings towards the ring haven't changed.'

Wazza cooked Coleen a candlelit dinner for their anniversary.

All the food was practically raw and covered in smoke.

Jamie Vardy met a woman who smiled at him.
'What's your name?' asked Jamie.
'Chantelle,' she said.
'Oh, go on, what is it?' he asked.

BOY: I've got you a present for our anniversary.

GIRL: Some gloves and a football shirt with a No. 1 on the back? Why on earth have you got me that?

BOY: Because you're a keeper.

Wazza was hoping to buy Coleen some perfume for Christmas, but he couldn't find anything expensive enough. He's got more money than scents.

KEEPER: My girlfriend's really clever. She has enough brains for two people.

DEFENDER: Then she's obviously the girl for you!

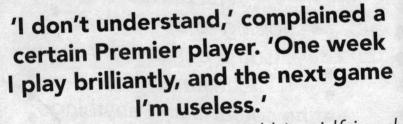

'I don't understand,' complained a certain Premier player. 'One week I play brilliantly, and the next game I'm useless.'

'I've got the answer,' said his girlfriend. 'Just play every other week.'

THE SWEETEST STARS
Sergio Agu-AERO
(Manchester City)
Lee KIT-KAT-termole *(Sunderland)*
MARS Bender *(Bayer Leverkusen)*
ROLO Toure *(Liverpool)*
John TERRY'S CHOCOLATE
ORANGE *(Chelsea)*

WHO'S GOOD ENOUGH TO EAT?
Bacary LASAGNE *(Manchester City)*
HAM SALAD-yce *(Sunderland)*
Francis COQ AU VIN *(Arsenal)*
PIZZA Crouch *(Stoke)*
Andy CARROT (*West Ham)*
Lionel ETON MESS-i *(Barcelona)*
CHOCOLATE MOUSSE-a
Dembele *(Tottenham)*
Alan MUTTON *(Aston Villa)*

BLOW THE WHISTLE

What do you call a referee with three eyes?

Seymour.

IF YOU HAVE A REFEREE IN FOOTBALL AND AN UMPIRE IN CRICKET, WHAT DO YOU HAVE IN BOWLS?
Goldfish.

What happened when the referee had a brain transplant?
The brain rejected him.

OPTICIAN: You'll be able to see the full length of the pitch with these new glasses.
REFEREE: That's wonderful! I never could with the old ones.

What do you call a referee wearing five balaclavas on a cold day?

Anything you like – he can't hear you.

'Did you say that the referee spreads happiness wherever he goes?'
'No, I said "whenever" he goes.'

'Off!' shouted the ref, blowing his whistle.
'Off? What for?' asked the player.
'For the rest of the match,' replied the ref.

Why did the referee have a sausage stuck behind his ear?

Because he'd eaten his whistle at lunchtime.

'Doctor! Come quickly! The referee has swallowed his pen! What can we do?'
'Use a pencil until I get there.'

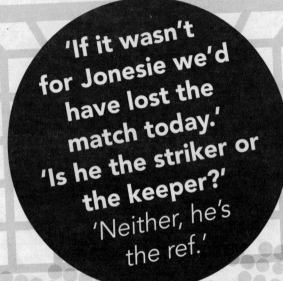

'If it wasn't for Jonesie we'd have lost the match today.'
'Is he the striker or the keeper?'
'Neither, he's the ref.'

THE DEVIL PROPOSED A FOOTBALL MATCH BETWEEN HEAVEN AND HELL. 'THAT WOULDN'T BE FAIR,' SAID AN IMP. 'HEAVEN HAS ALL THE FOOTBALLERS.' 'I KNOW,' REPLIED THE DEVIL. 'BUT WE HAVE ALL THE REFEREES.'

Did you hear about the referee who was so short-sighted he couldn't go to sleep unless he counted elephants?

Did you hear about the referee who got so fed up with the poor players in the teams playing that he awarded a free kick to himself?

The referee was showing his friends his new stopwatch. 'It's an amazing watch,' he said. 'It only cost fifty p.'
'Why is it so amazing?'
'Because every time I look at it I'm amazed it's still working.'

One day when United were playing the referee didn't turn up, so the captain asked if there was anyone among the spectators with refereeing experience.

A man stepped forward.

'Have you refereed before?' asked the captain.

'Certainly,' said the man. 'And if you don't believe me ask my three friends here.'

'I'm sorry,' said the captain. 'But I don't think we can use you.'

'Why not?'

'You can't be a real referee – no real referee has three friends.'

REFEREE:
I didn't come here to
be insulted!
FAN:
Where do you
usually go?

CLUBCALL

CHRISTMAS CRACKERS

SNOW Hart *(Manchester City)*

SANTA Cazorla *(Arsenal)*

JESUS Navas *(Manchester City)*

Kurt SATSUMA *(Chelsea)*

SLEIGH-ton Baines *(Everton)*

Mamadou SACK-ho
(Liverpool)

Memphis De-MINCE PIE
(Manchester United)

Harry CANDY CANE
(Tottenham)

Philippe Coutin-HO HO HO
(Liverpool)

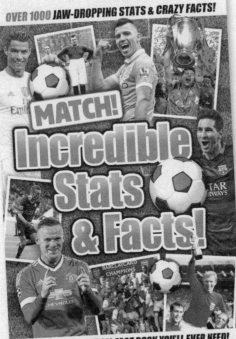

OVER 1000 JAW-DROPPING STATS & CRAZY FACTS

from the makers of the UK's best football magazine! Includes brilliant lists and records, from fastest goals to top scorers and most red cards to tallest stars in the Premier League. And also amazing player facts, bonkers football injuries, biggest transfer fees, fantastic footy legends, trophy trivia, stunning stadiums, incredible strange-but-true revelations, all the firsts, and the fastest, tallest, boldest facts about the Champions League, the Premier League, the FA Cup, the UEFA European Championship and the World Cup.